TEDDY & ME

TEDDY & ME

CONFESSIONS OF A SERVICE HUMAN

MICHAEL SAVAGE

PHOTOGRAHY BY VINCENT REMINI

CENTER
STREET

All photographs copyright © Vincent Remini.

Book design by Timothy Shaner, NightandDayDesign.biz

CENTER STREET
Hachette Book Group
1290 Avenue of the Americas
New York, NY 10104

www.CenterStreet.com

Printed in the United States of America

WOR

First edition: May 2016

10 9 8 7 6 5 4 3 2 1

Center Street is a division of Hachette Book Group, Inc.

The Center Street name and logo are trademarks of Hachette Book Group, Inc.

The Hachette Speakers Bureau provides a wide range of authors for speaking events.
To find out more, go to www.HachetteSpeakersBureau.com or call (866) 376-6591.

The publisher is not responsible for websites (or their content) that are not owned by the publisher.

Library of Congress Control Number: 2016934148

ISBN: 978-1-4555-3612-2

CONTENTS

1. YOU CAN JUDGE PEOPLE BY
   HOW THEY TREAT DOGS 11

2. BEST FRIENDS 23

3. TEDDY IS MY COPILOT 33

4. JEROME 47

5. KINDLY DOGS & KINDLY BEARS 57

6. TIPPY & ALL MY OTHER DOGS 63

7. TEDDY INSPIRES ME 79

8. PERSPECTIVE 99

9. TEDDY EATS OUT 109

10. MOMENTS TO CHERISH 119

For Janet
Who Brought Him
Into My Life

TEDDY & ME

YOU CAN JUDGE PEOPLE BY HOW THEY TREAT DOGS

Let's go fishing!

All aboard!

1.

A neighbor recently said to me that he judges a man by how he treats dogs. I said, "Oh, I agree with that." In fact, I think it was a famous writer who wrote that in those places where we go after we pass, when we get there our pets are the masters and we're the pets. How we treated our pets is how they treat us in those two places. I kind of like that. Now, that's not the reason that I treat my pets so well, but nevertheless, it's nice to hedge your bets.

Well, my neighbor and I were also talking about the famous Teddy story, of when he tried to rescue an ocean swimmer. Oh, yes. Now, Teddy is a little guy—he's only eleven pounds. He doesn't know how big he is or how small he is. Little dogs are like that. Being a purebred poodle, he is still in great shape—really great shape. About a year ago, he disappeared, and I thought he had drowned. You see, I live next to San Francisco Bay, in a small house right on the breakwater. I usually watch Teddy like a hawk. One day

15

I looked around and yelled for him, but he was gone. He was nowhere to be found.

I panicked and thought that he had accidentally jumped in the water or had fallen in and drowned. I went up and down my street asking all my neighbors, "Have you seen Teddy?"

Everyone said they hadn't seen him. My heart dropped. I thought, my God, what do I do now? I took my eye off him for a minute and he's gone, I don't know how I'm going to live with this one. Soon enough a man, another neighbor who swims in the bay, came walking down the street in his bathing suit. He had been swimming off my breakwater that morning.

A middle-aged man, and strong, he said to me, "My God, that dog of yours is some wild animal."

I said, "What do you mean?"

He said, "I thought that dog was a poof dog. He is so macho."

I repeated, "What do you mean?"

He said, "Didn't you hear what happened?"

I said, "No."

He said, "Well, I swim by your breakwater every morning. Teddy was out there and he jumped in the water and he swam out to me. He put his face right next to mine, looked me right in the eye, as if to say, "Are you okay?" And then he swam back to the breakwater at an angle. As I continued to swim, he would jump

Are you okay?

"I'm sorry, Dad, I just had to do it. It's in my blood."

in the water every ten or fifteen feet, swim out to me, swim up to my face and check me out to make sure I was okay. Then he would swim back to the breakwater, run down the rocks on the breakwater some, and continue onward down for about a quarter mile, where it ended."

I said, "Oh my God, well, I don't know where the dog is." I went to the back of the house, which actually sits on the bay, and lo and behold, here comes little old Teddy Trueheart, covered with seaweed, full of mud, running down the seawall looking up at me and with his eyes, "I'm sorry, Dad, I just had to do it. It's in my blood." That's the famous Teddy story, probably the best one, and it's 100 percent true.

I told my neighbor that story the other day when he was telling me about how he judges a man by how he treats dogs.

I said, "You do know that Muslims hate dogs, don't you?"

19

He said, "What?"

I said, "You don't remember that famous story when the Somalis were brought into Minneapolis as refugees? Many of them became cabdrivers? About ten years ago? When they wouldn't even take a blind person in their cab, saying, 'Dogs are filthy, get out of my cab.' You don't remember that?"

His face dropped with horror, this dog-loving friend of mine.

I guess you can say you can judge a person by how they treat dogs.

Thanks for the reward!

BEST
FRIENDS

2.

WELL, Teddy is my best friend, there's no question about it. Everything I do, he does. I don't have to spell it out. Anyone who owns a dog knows how attached they become to your every habit, from the bathroom to the car. Let's leave it at that. Now, we can say that dog is man's best friend, and he is, but let's not forget that dogs are not human beings. Some would say that they are better than human beings. In some ways I guess you could say that, but humans are different from dogs or any other animal.

I guess I have to repeat that because we've forgotten what a human being really is.

I remember, for example, when I was a boy, maybe ten or eleven or twelve, and I had a best friend. We will call him Steven. And waking up on Saturday mornings hasn't felt like that—the days of boyhood—since. The whole day waited for us. Usually it consisted of getting on our bicycles and going on a very long ride. There used to be a bicycle path where I grew up in Queens, New York. They said it was Vanderbilt's private roadway for his racing car. I don't know whether that was true or not, but it was an amazing place to take a bike ride. We'd start out in mid-Queens

where I lived, sort of in the Jamaica area, actually near Donald Trump's house, just on the other side of Union Turnpike—the main roadway that separates the houses of the lower-middle from the upper-middle classes—and we'd bicycle all day long, way, way out. Sometimes we'd be gone all day, talking, playing, kidding, laughing.

Now how can you compare that with the companionship of an animal, even a highly intelligent, intuitive dog? I ask this not to diminish my relationship with Teddy or any of my other dogs,

Teddy instructs me on a finer point in regard to this complex Ferrari engine.

Teddy walks away from the job. He threw in the towel.

"He's always been my friend and he's always been there for me. That will never change."

which have all been special, but to keep things in perspective. Man is unique, special in all kinds of ways, some of which are even negative. Still, having said that, there is no more consistently loyal friend than a dog. See, I don't know that friend Steven anymore. We were friends as boys, and then as adolescents we were still friends. But, as we became men, we went our own ways. We found out we were very different and had nothing in common.

The same can't be said for a relationship with a dog. In this sense, for the eleven or twelve years I've been with Teddy so far, it's been a very consistent relationship. He's always been my friend and he's always been there for me. That will never change. This, of course, leads to the inevitable question of eternity, which I do not think is a question I can address at this time.

Darn, those triple carbs
are complicated, Teddy.

TEDDY
IS MY
COPILOT

It's show business with
Teddy the movie star!

3.

I BELIEVE IN GOD, but when I'm driving, Teddy is my copilot. He reflects my attitudes and instincts and sometimes guides them. You see, most of the time we live outside the city so he has a little grassy lawn to run on and a grassy hill to play on. When we're in the little cottage on the bay he likes the gulls and cormorants, the seals, and other sea creatures right off our back deck. On days he's not feeling well, as his service human, I hold him in my arms and point out the "birdies," as we call them, diving for fish or the occasional moldy bagel I throw into the bay.

He sits by my side watching each and every radio show. In fact, I'll bet he knows more about politics than any dog in the world, even the Obamas'

dog. After awhile he gets bored so, for fun, he nips at the engineer's sneakers when he comes over to tweak my equipment. At least once a week, I drive him over the Golden Gate Bridge to San Francisco. We head to my high-rise apartment downtown. I refer to the building's elevator as the "Tedevator" because his eyes widen with anticipation at the thought of this marvelous, gravity-defying machine that whisks us up to the twentieth floor, where he can stare down at the bay, boats, and people.

But I'm getting ahead of my story about being the most grateful service human in America. The minute we get over the bridge, Teddy stands up and starts gaping at all the people in the streets. He loves when I have to stop at a traffic light on Lombard Street so he can see the flow of humans, the stores, the restaurants, even the cars next to us. I know he's starved for stimulation. Those gulls and seals have their limits. Anyway, when we hit the garage in the building, he's first out to the Tedevator!

What show prep Ted, way to go.

I need a nap!

Give me a break
Dad, things
aren't that bad!

Are you kidding? That's what Obama said?

Dad, put that book down and lets' go for a walk!

JEROME

4.

I'M not a particularly religious man. I was raised in an atheistic household. My father was an atheist from Russia and my mother was a kind of very faithful believer. Not religious, per se, but she really knew God existed. She did things that made me know that. The way she dealt with the tragedy of my silent brother taught me many things. The way my father dealt with it was another. The way I deal with it is another. I learned to be an entertainer because of my mother's sadness and tragedy.

My mother was deeply saddened by what happened to my brother. And she couldn't fathom what happened—she didn't know why. She had a healthy daughter, then a healthy son, me, then she had another boy who looked perfectly fine—blonde hair, blue eyes, perfectly fine. And then in a short period of time, they found out he was not normal—couldn't see, couldn't hear, couldn't speak. He was basically a vegetable, so they thought. Well, it wrecked the whole family. My mother would cry endlessly in the apartment. No one knew this. What does a little boy do when a mother is crying? He tries to make her happy. So I would entertain her. I would do stupid things. I became an entertainer

> *"I also learned how to talk to audiences and animals because of my silent brother."*

for my mother. I would imitate people. I'd put on faces. I would make sounds and noises and I'd wipe the tears away. She'd stop crying. She would smile.

Even my closest family members didn't know this story. I learned to talk to silent audiences and to entertain because of the tragedy with my brother. You say, "Ah, what's the big deal? People die every day. Stop talkin' about it so much." All right. Just telling you how one man's soul operates.

So it affected me in that I learned to entertain my mother. As a result, I can go from the maudlin to the enraged man in one second. In one second I can turn from a kind of maudlin, sad guy into an enraged bull—in one second. It all rages inside my soul and in that sense I'm very much alive, top to bottom.

But I also learned how to talk to audiences and animals because of my silent brother. They said, "Don't talk to him." He was sitting in a highchair, strapped in there. He was blind, he was deaf, and he couldn't speak. And when no one was looking, I would sneak into the kitchen to talk to him. I want you to see how primitive the world was in the 1940s in the doctors' profession. So they told me,

the healthy brother, "Don't go in there—don't talk to your brother. You'll bother him." I said, "What do you mean? How can I bother him if he can't hear me?" So I would talk to him anyway because I loved him. I just loved him so much. And I would whistle to him because I didn't think he could understand words. And he would smile when I whistled to him. So I thought, wait a minute, if he can understand the whistle, he knows his brother's here. And then I hear the voice: "Michael? Michael, what are you doing in there? Are you bothering Jerome? Come on, get out of there."

Then he was left alone to die in a snake pit of a state-run hospital. The doctors decided that, for the sake of the healthy children, they're going to give him away to a home. I want you to think

about the profound impact on the "healthy children," that we were responsible for sending him to hell.

So the day he was taken away is forever branded in my mind. It's important to remember I was born in the 1940s. There was no television. It was the age of radio. The whole thing's set around radio. See, it's why I'm so able on the radio. I grew up in the age of radio. That's why I am who I am on the radio. That's why I do things no one else dares do on the radio, because I am radio. I come from the age of radio. I'm pre-television.

The day came that they had to give him away to a state home. It was a horrible place on Staten Island. A snake pit that, years later, was shown to be a horrible, decrepit place. You think the VA hospitals are bad? They took this little, five-year-old helpless boy and, because the doctors were such quacks in those days, they took him away in the streets.

Now, in those days, everyone knew everyone. I lived in a tenement in the Bronx. Six, eight stories—I don't know what it was. Everybody knew everybody. It was like a Satyajit Ray movie. If you've ever watched Indian movies about India, Calcutta, the teeming masses, well, that's my childhood. So those are the days when, if you watch retro movies, you see women sitting outside in front of the building in chairs. The children are playing in the streets. In the summer they'd open up the fire hydrants so the kids could run in the cold water to cool off. That was our swimming pool—it was the gutter and the water. It felt good to me. I enjoyed it. It was cold—and fresh. And the women would protect you from any, you know, potential harm. They all sat on folding chairs next to the buildings and watched the children. But there was little potential danger there because nobody would speed down the street. There were no guns going off, and the perverts would be thrown off the top of a building if they were caught. If there was even a hint of a perv in a neighborhood, the men would find him and they would either beat him up or throw him off a building. So we had a very, very good childhood in that sense.

So everyone knew everyone. And the day comes. They hear that they're giving away the boy. Everybody is in the street. *Everybody* is in the street. There's crying. There's sadness. And the whole neighborhood sees this going on. My little brother is taken away. Two men in white. And that was the beginning of something and it was also the end of something.

What am I supposed to believe? That God made a mistake? It was just a mistake in the hospital? Somebody made a mistake somewhere and they did this to him? Or it was a neurological defect that created my brother and there was no reason for him?

Well, I actually think he was created like that for me. I believe that my brother was created that way for me to be as articulate as I am and as impassioned as I am. And in that sense, I'm very guilty. I have to live for two people. I've told you that before. Otherwise, there's no explanation for me to be alive this long—not with my genetic inheritance, not with the stress level I've lived with. I should've been dead a long time ago. I think that Jerry had to suffer for me to live the way I am. Would you believe this? And that's the sad story of how I learned to communicate with audiences and animals from my silent brother.

KINDLY DOGS
&
KINDLY BEARS

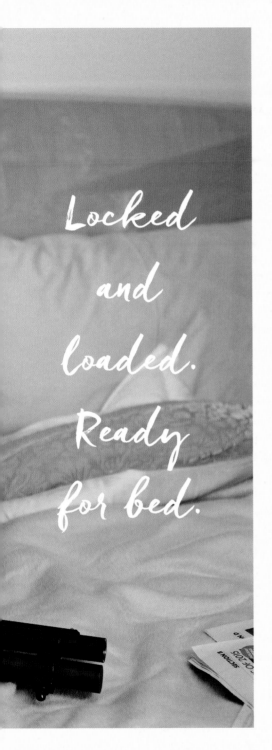

Locked
and
loaded.
Ready
for bed.

5.

HERE'S a bedtime story I wrote and read to Ted some rainy nights when the thunder scares him . . .

I n the forest, there lived some bears, but they were a lost tribe of little bears—very little bears. Whenever someone passed by they hid and so no one had ever seen them.

In the village, there were hunting dogs, big hunting dogs that hated bears. They were called poodles. Everyone thought they were cute because they smiled as poodles do. But they were bred to hunt, not to smile.

In this village there was a kindly old man who loved both dogs and bears. He cried every

time the hunters came home with a bear, so he decided to help both bears and dogs. First he found the smallest of the poodles. Then he secretly married the little poodle to another little poodle, and they had seven small baby poodles.

Then he went back into the forest and found an abandoned baby bear that was left behind after his mama was taken by the hunters. He took the baby bear home and introduced her to the small baby poodles. They all played together in Mr. Kindly's cottage.

Then one day, the old man thought, "What's going to happen to them when I'm gone? Who will take care of them?" Mr. Kindly decided he would keep choosing from the smallest of these little bears and the smallest of these dogs and help them have babies.

Years later, when Mr. Kindly was gone, and his small cottage sat abandoned in the deep forest, a group of

schoolchildren on a field trip stumbled upon it. They slowly tiptoed in. As they looked around, they found torn and yellowed scraps of pictures showing the kindly old man surrounded by little dogs and little bears, all cozy together around a warm fire in the hearth.

The children's teacher wondered where all those cute furry animals came from, and where they went.

Deep in the forest there was a huge, huge tree whose trunk was wider than an elephant. It was more than two hundred years old. In this tree was a little door carved near the foot of the trunk. This door led to a cave, which spread out forever and a mile, and only God in heaven could see where this endless cave led.

Somewhere beyond this tree, there is a world where tiny bears and tiny poodles sit together sipping on honeyed leaves no human has ever seen, that give all the nutrition needed for kindly bears and kindly dogs to live forever and a day.

THE END.

TIPPY & ALL MY OTHER DOGS

Jumping for joy!

5.

TIPPY

I've had dogs all my life. My first dog was Tippy, a part chow with purple blotches on his tongue. He was a pretty rough customer. In fact, I have scars to the bone on my left leg reminding me of Tippy. When he was a small puppy and I was a small boy, I was teasing him a bit on a hot August day in the Catskill Mountains in New York. You see, I took a bone that was given to him and I ground it into the dirt with my left foot as I looked at him mischievously. Well, he didn't like it, so he leapt at my foot and sank his teeth in, right down to my bone. Well, after that they rushed me to the hospital and stitched me up. I thought it was quite an experience. I actually enjoyed the whole deal. I didn't feel any pain. Then they called my father, who was at work in New York City, and they told him what happened. He closed up his store and he got in his car and drove the two and a half hours up to the mountains. And being the Solomonic father that he was, he asked me in great detail what had happened. You see, all the men had said they should put the dog to sleep. Everyone was saying, "That dog's no good. He's gotta be put to sleep." But my

father, as I said, being quite judicial, asked me exactly what happened. So I said, "Well, Dad, I can't lie." I told him about grinding the bone into the dirt. Well, at that moment, Tippy's life was no longer in jeopardy. And that's the best story I remember about Tippy.

Tippy was quite a wild animal throughout the rest of his life, especially when someone came to visit my parents—and they had loads of friends who would stop in at all times unannounced. That's how it was in those days. It was a very close-knit community. There was no standing on ceremony with my mother. People would just show up. Well, she had to lock Tippy in the basement. He'd go crazy barking and banging the front door. He was just a ferocious little lion. So she'd yell at him and chase him into the little doorway that led down to our basement and lock him in there. And he'd stay down there and bang on that door until they left.

One day my dad's friends and her friends were sitting around having coffee and cake, talking as they did, and my father said, "Okay, let him out. He won't hurt anybody." Well, he came out and the first thing he did was run up to the fattest guy in the crowd. His name was

George and he was a bookie of some kind. George the bookie weighed three hundred pounds and had a twenty-five-inch neck, and was always jolly, always laughing, at least on the outside. He had had a lot of tragedy in his life. Tippy ran right up to George, jumped on his leg, and fell in love with his lower calf, if you know what I mean. Well, my mother went crazy with the broom. She started to beat him and scream, "You dirty dog! Get off George's foot!"

As you can imagine the entire crowd broke up in laughter until she finally beat Tippy off George's leg and chased him back into the dungeon.

The last Tippy story is of his death—and, as you might expect, it's kind of sad. Years later, the dog was around nine and he had a horrible diet. There was no kibble. He was fed Ken-L Ration, which was probably bad horsemeat and table scraps. Well, one day we came downstairs and there he was, lying as stiff as a board at the bottom of the steps. My mother started to cry and we didn't know what to do. My father wasn't home. So she called the New York City Department of Sanitation. Well, they came over with a garbage truck and two somber-faced, brown-suited garbagemen came into our

little attached house in Queens, looked at us—somberly—and carted Tippy out. One of the garbagemen was holding his front paws, the other his back feet. And as God is my witness, when they got to the garbage truck, they started the machine going—the conveyor that takes in the trash—and with a one-two-three they heaved Tippy into the back. So long, Tippy.

WOODY/WILLY

The next two dogs I owned, way before Teddy, were the cutest little things in the world. One was a Yorkie named Woody, I believe. I mix up Woody and Willy. The other, Willy, was a silky terrier. They were the spunkiest, eternally moving little fur machines I've ever seen. I don't remember much about them except how they both left this earth. I don't know whether you want to hear this story or not, but here we go.

I was walking with little Woody in Forest Hills, Queens, and from across the street there came a spotted Dalmatian that ran at him like a wolf. Before I could even lift a finger or raise my voice the Dalmatian snapped his jaws shut around Woody's little back, punctured his lungs, and killed him in front of my eyes. Well, I

"He'd run out of our house, run down the hill, run across the valley, and up the other side to a house where there was a female dog he took a liking to. He was so smart that he knew how to open the gate with his teeth and let her out."

didn't know if he was dead or not, but I grabbed Woody, jumped in my little old Volkswagen, a little green Beetle, and raced over the Queensboro Bridge to an animal hospital, where the vet announced that Woody was dead.

Well, okay. Things happen. Terrible things. To this day I'm afraid to walk a small dog in the streets anywhere in America for fear that a big dog will kill him. Maybe it's a good thing to be this protective.

The other dog, Willy, was just the most charming little guy, and I had him when I lived in Hawaii. That dog also came to a weird and sad end. We had been away on a short trip and we were supposed to come back on a certain day. We left him in the good care of a wonderful, kindly friend, who was a botanist. Well, we came back a day later than we'd planned, and on the day we were supposed to come back but didn't, little Willy had eaten a teeny poisonous frog and died. We buried him there in Hawaii. I still know where, in the back of Manoa Valley near a waterfall. It's the way of all flesh. And that's the story of Woody and Willy.

BANDIT

The next dog story is about a wild border collie named Bandit. This is a beautiful story. Bandit was the dog that we owned when we were living in Fairfax, California, while the children were quite young. In those days I used to go into San Francisco quite a lot, either by car or by ferry. One day I took the ferry from a suburban town called Larkspur, which happens to be adjacent to San Quentin Prison. When inmates are released from San Quentin, they're given bus fare, and some of them take the ferry into San Francisco and go home. Well, on that particular day—it was a rainy day, if I remember it, in November—I was almost alone on this huge ferry, and there was a long-haired guy who had just been released from prison. I could tell by his look

How's that Dad?

All four feet
off the ground.

that he was a hardened criminal. But since I'm attracted to antisocial types, he and I struck up a conversation, liked each other, and he invited me to his house. I said, "Oh boy, this is great."

He told me he had indeed just gotten out of San Quentin, though I didn't ask him what he'd been in for. We got off the ferry and took some buses for an hour to South San Francisco, near Candlestick Park, and walked across boards on a mud flat way out to some houseboat. His "old lady" was there and she was the nicest person in the world. They had a houseful of dogs. We drank all afternoon, and he offered me one of the dogs. How could I say no to an ex–Hell's Angel from San Quentin? Get the picture? So I took the little dog in my arm, put him in my coat, walked back on the planks, took the bus back to the ferry, and took the dog home.

The children fell in love with him. Oh, he was a border collie all right, and a wild one, one of the wildest dogs we ever owned. As the years when on, Bandit would constantly try to escape from the house. He'd run out of our house, run down the hill, run across the valley, and up the other side to a house where there was a female dog he took a liking to. He was so smart that he knew how to open the gate with his teeth and let her out. Then they would run together all afternoon. True story.

They liked the state park area way up on Mount Tamalpais. One day a park ranger came to our house with Bandit in tow and said to us, "Your dog is chasing down deer up in the mountain with this other dog and he does it all the time. And if he does it one more time, I'm gonna shoot him." How's that for a nice, sensitive animal control agent? Well, we kept Bandit under control, because we didn't want a mean park ranger to shoot him.

Years later I was teaching at an East Coast college. We had crossed the country like in *The Grapes of Wrath* with all of our possessions, rented a house, and I taught for a while. Well, we used to chain Bandit to a large tree in front of the house because we didn't want to chain him up inside. Well, sad to say, one day the kids came home from middle school and the chain was there, but Bandit was gone. We had all sorts of stories as to what happened. He escaped the chain, ran off, and found another female dog, and he's running happily ever after, or a group of evil people cut the chain and stole him and he came to God knows what end. Either way, that was the end of Bandit.

SNOWY

Snowy was a sheltie and she was the kindest, most beautiful dog I ever owned. She preceded Teddy. Snowy was our little Lassie. She was with us all through our kids' childhood years. And I always remember Snowy jumping over little fences. You know, sort of the Rebecca of Sunnybrook Farm type of thing. She had that kind of disposition. She was obviously a female and I think she was the only female dog I ever owned. I can't remember another female dog. I always liked little boy dogs. But Snowy was just the sweetest little Lassie you could ever know and all the memories are fantastic. Even to the end she was a wonderful dog and a great inspiration.

She was in great health until the age of eleven or twelve. Unfortunately her downfall was due to my overfeeding her. I can't

"Snowy was our little Lassie. She was with us all through our kids' childhood years. And I always remember Snowy jumping over little fences."

help it. If I eat, she sits there, looks at me, and I feed her. And I let her gain too much weight. She got fat and she got sick. She got arthritis, and I couldn't care for her anymore. Well, luckily for me, my personal assistant at that time had a girlfriend whose parents were dog lovers who lived on a farm up in Sonoma County, California, north of San Francisco. They agreed to take Snowy in for her last years. She wasn't supposed to last too long. In fact, the vet had told us that we were supposed to put her to sleep, and I said, "My friend, no one's putting Snowy to sleep."

But the story ends beautifully because these nice people up in Sonoma put Snowy on a special diet, limited her food intake, and she lived another two years. And then they called two years later and said, "She's near the end."

I remember going up there and getting down on the grass with her. I looked in her eyes though she could hardly see. She was lying there and I whistled to her as I did to my brother. We talked. I told her who I was and I told her I loved her, and I left.

She passed away the next day. Now, the beautiful part of this story is that she actually predeceased my mother, who was very sick in a nursing home in Florida at the time. And I think that God, you know, kind of got me ready for what was coming through the passage of this beautiful friend of mine.

Our favorite pastime. What could be better—the clicker and Ted.

TEDDY
INSPIRES ME

Let's gor for
a bike ride!

6.

SINCE so much of talk radio is based upon anger and rage and even hatred sometimes, and indignation, I often turn to my best friend Teddy to feel kindness, warmth, and love. He inspires me to feel these things. And that's why it's important to have my dog at my side during almost every show. My voice and my ability to move crowds are my gift, but also my burden. This power of the magical voice, which I first discovered in the first grade in a slum school in the Bronx, can change people's fates. How would you use this power as a broadcaster and bestselling author if you were me? I intend to make this day the first day of the rest of my life, as people used to say in the hippie sixties and seventies. We can change our lives. You say, "What's wrong with your life, Michael?" Well, it's not that there's anything wrong with my life, but it's not what I want it to be. I don't feel that I'm inspiring people in the way I want to inspire them. You see, you can inspire through hate, as ISIS does, as the ACLU does, even as Hillary and Obama do in their own quasi-moderate ways. They inspire through hate. You can inspire through anger. You can inspire through rage. You can inspire through false righteous indignation. We know that's all out there. We get it every day of the week, mainly on talk radio. In varieties, that's what you get. Anger, rage, false righteous indignation. And it riles you up and you listen. That's an inspiration.

But then there's the bigger inspirations. You can inspire through love, hope, humor. The positives. I know it sounds hippie-dippy sixties, but I look at the history of the world and I look at the world today and I realize that if we don't inspire each other through positive attributes we're going to descend into the barbarism of the left and the barbarism of ISIS.

Now, maybe this is a different turn for Michael Savage. I get it. You like me to be hard. You like me to be tough. You like me to be cynical. You like me to be analytical. I get that. But there's a limit to that. Believe it or not, that's all limited. There's a lot of area beyond all that. It's called space, time, and the universe, and I want to go there. I want to go there in this life with you and I want to inspire you in the most positive manner.

I think about the Christmas season, the season of peace and the season of love. Christianity is the religion of peace. Christianity is the true religion of peace. Islam is not a religion of peace. Christianity is. Turn the other cheek. Do unto others as you would have them do unto you. These are messages that come from Christianity. What can you do in an age of deceit and lies and terror? What you can do is reaffirm your own religion. Instead of letting your church become a mosque or a Unitarian meeting place or a drunk tank on Tuesday nights, you can go to church again. However hokey that sounds, however cynical you are, however hard you are, however unneeding you think you really are, you know in your heart that there's something missing in you. You know that you crave something greater. Because the human being is not a dog. The human being is not a bear. The human being is not a snake. The human being is not an eagle. We are unique creatures and we need something different than the bear, the dog, the snake, and the eagle. What is it? It's the thing called God. These creatures, they don't know God. They are of God. They were created by God. But they don't really need God. That's why they're lower animals. We as higher animals need higher things than just food and fornication. Unfortunately, our society—primarily because of the degenerates in the media—has fallen lower than the snake. The media has promulgated the idea that we only need food and fornication. And so when people are empty, that's what they seek: food and fornication. And when they're really empty, what happens? They become drug addicts. They start with marijuana. They end up with heroin, crack, you name it. What is it about drugs? What is it that human beings are seeking in drugs? Why do they go for drugs? As God has been driven out of America, drugs have entered.

Wheelin' away.

"There's a lot of area beyond all that. It's called space, time, and the universe, and I want to go there. I want to go there in this life with you and I want to inspire you in the most positive manner."

I know this has been said before. I get it. But what does an empty soul look to do? An empty soul looks to fill itself, just as an empty vessel needs to be filled with a liquid to be complete. An empty human being needs to fill himself to be complete. And how does it fill itself? I know again many of you will laugh because you're cynical. It's through those things I'm talking about. Inspiration. The musician finds the inspiration God knows where and then has the inspiration to pick up the instrument. Do you think a musician can play one day without inspiration from somewhere? Unfortunately, so many musicians don't have that human inspiration that they seek, and they get it through drugs. I get that. I understand. It's true for many artists who don't understand that the greatest artists were not drug addicts. The greatest artists in

87

the history of the world were not drug addicts. They were usually God addicts. Did you know that? Look at the greatest art in history. You'll find it was created by super-religious people who literally saw God in their living rooms. The power of God was transmitted through the paintbrush or through that piece of marble. How could a man like Rodin take a piece of inert stone and see the essence of a human form and sculpt—from inside that stone, that block of marble—the portrait of a human being that looks so real that a hundred years later I can go to the museum and look at it and inside that carved eye I can literally see the person? How is that possible? How?

So I say it again. My voice and my ability to move crowds are my gifts. But they are also my burden. This is a power, the magical voice. It's a power I first discovered when I found out I could speak to the assembly in the first grade at PS 48 in a slum school in the Bronx. I found out that I enjoyed speaking to that crowd of kids. I wasn't afraid of them. I loved seeing them smile when I told a joke or made a fool of myself. It didn't matter. I was a little clown and they laughed. I liked that. When I spoke with such a clear voice and wasn't afraid, the little pipsqueak that I was, and the crowd listened to me, I enjoyed that power, and I discovered something. I discovered I can move audiences and that means I can change people's fates, as I learned later in life.

On the road...

"It's not about just being a clown. It's not about entertaining people and making them laugh. It's about changing people's fates. It's a great gift and a great burden."

It's not about just being a clown. It's not about entertaining people and making them laugh. It's about changing people's fates. It's a great gift and a great burden. Yeah, I said it again and I'll repeat it again. Some inspire through hate. Do I have to say who? Do I have to mention who inspires through hate and division? Do I have to say the names or the organizations that use hate and division—not to mention anger, rage, false righteous indignation—as their stock-in-trade? I've used all of them. In my twenty-one years on the radio, I've used every one of those emotions to move my audiences. Because every one of those emotions raged through me or played through me, or danced through me.

You can inspire in other ways. You can inspire through love, hope, and humor. But how do you do that? All right, so I talk about the dog, and many of you love Teddy. Today I'm very angry at him because he peed on the floor again when I turned my back. I got very mad at him. It was two minutes before the show. Two minutes. He snuck in the room that he goes in and he did it. I got so angry. I had to be on my hands and knees with a spray bottle and a piece of paper two minutes before a national show. As I was cleaning up this dog's mess I got so mad at him for sneaking around and doing that that I actually started to laugh. And I said, "You know, I remember way back in the seventies some friends of mine who were Buddhists used to go to some of these Buddhists meetings where there were some very, very wise teachers. And there was one of the teachers in particular that all of the white guys would go and sit before with their legs crossed in the lotus position, looking for some great inspiration. And sometimes they'd get these really wacky statements, such as "Take the garbage out if you wanna know what it is to be a Buddhist. Because if you don't take your own garbage out, you can't be an ascended master." They didn't even understand what he was saying to them. What he was saying to them is don't get so disconnected from reality that you don't even know what you are. In other words, don't leave your body. And if that means taking your own garbage out, then do it.

There's a similar story about Albert Einstein. At this point he was quite famous and he had agreed to a meeting with some man.

Love that air!

"You cannot let the cynical times that we are living in deprive you of your humanity. Because if you lose your humanity, you're going to lose everything."

Einstein was sitting behind his desk and the visitor said, "Herr Einstein, Herr Einstein, I realize what your theory of relativity means. It means that nothing is real. Nothing is real." As the story goes, Einstein stood up slowly, walked over to him, and slapped him in the face. And he said, "Is that real?"

Now do you see what I'm saying to you? Don't let your philosophy disconnect you from reality or you might put yourself in danger. That might mean slipping on a sidewalk because your head is in the clouds or bicycling through an intersection and killing a civilian because you think you're invincible, as occurs too often in San Francisco, where there are no laws against these bicycle terrorists. There are in fact many other ways you can get so disconnected from your body that you have no reality, which leads us back to the question of how can I inspire in an age where those who hate us want to kill us and in fact are killing us. The word *inspire* has in it everything I want to say. Inspire. Inspire. To give you courage, to give you hope, to give you strength, to give you wisdom. That's what inspire means to me.

How many times have I gone into a house of worship in my life and walked out feeling emptier than when I went in? That's why religion is dying in America. It's not growing. I would go into these houses of worship in the emptiest times of my life and come out feeling worse than before. Do you know why? Because there was no leadership, just like the political class. You go in there, you hear mumbo jumbo and weakness. You don't want that. You want fire and brimstone. You want a man to get up there and lead you out of your darkness into the light, don't you?

Where does inspiration come from? Anger, rage, and false righteous indignation. Okay, fine. You can be inspired by all those things. But then you lose your humanity. That's the whole point I'm trying to make. You cannot let the cynical times that we are living in deprive you of your humanity. Because if you lose your humanity, you're going to lose everything. Even if you survive physically, you will die spiritually.

PERSPECTIVE

Teddy's favorite: chicken!

7.

HE does not live in my house. It is Teddy's house. And I am there to serve him. It explains most of a domesticated pet's behavior, when you think about it.

China produces most dog "treats," and so many deaths have been traced to toxins in these horrible pieces of dried duck feet and other garbage nobody would eat. I feed Teddy freshly cooked chicken, carrots, and kibble each and every day. And because he grew up in a Basque restaurant enjoying sirloin, he just won't eat jerky.

Whenever we're out and I mention his name, strangers turn and stare.

"He's Teddy?" they say. "So you must be Michael—Michael Savage!"

"Yes," I answer, if they don't look like killers, and add, "I'm Teddy's service human."

Chicken, again?

What's that vintage
in dog years?

Those
old guys
sure had
an eye.

Portrait of Ted by Savage

Self Portrait of a Service Human

TEDDY
EATS OUT

At last! Relief has arrived.

9.

TEDDY grew up frequenting a Basque restaurant near where I live. Now you say, what is he doing in a restaurant? Well, there's a couple of reasons he's always eaten there:

Number one, in France, dogs are permitted in restaurants.

Number two, the owner is a man who loves animals, who loves me, and loves my work, and Teddy is never a problem. He has always been a quiet dog, he never barks, he never messes, he's grown up eating some of my food. I always order a hamburger, no salt, no pepper and give him half of it, chopped up with a little cold water. He enjoys a little Bordeaux red wine from the tip of my finger, never more than one lick, but he sure enjoys his wine! As the years have gone on, Teddy and I have eaten in several restaurants. He doesn't bother anybody. In fact, the people bother him more than he bothers anyone else. There's not much I can say about it other than, if most people's dogs behaved the way Teddy does in restaurants, I would have no problem with people bringing dogs into restaurants. But that's not the norm. The norm is

"Teddy is a part of me—
I'm a part of him."

that dogs bark, they pee, and they disturb other people in restaurants. And that's why it's generally a good rule to not have dogs in restaurants. We don't feed Teddy from the porcelain dishes, we feed him from paper plates that are disposed of, just in case you're interested. The reason I take him and I leave the other dogs at home is because of the way Teddy was trained. I don't know if I've said this before, but if poodles are left home alone, they sulk for days, they become heartbroken—they literally want to be with you 24/7. Teddy is that kind of dog. Some are like this, some aren't. If you go in the shower, he's sitting next to the shower pulling guard duty. You go to sleep, he's next to the bed or at the foot of your bed. Well, that's how Teddy is. Teddy is a part of me—I'm a part of him.

It's number two Teddy!
And away we go.

Ted, I'm feelin' no pain!

And to all a good night!
(Ted, did you call Uber?)

MOMENTS TO CHERISH

Let's go for a walk!

Come on Toby,
let's get in shape.

10.

I'VE owned many dogs but of all my animals I'm closest to Teddy, and I came to know it even more so this year when he had to go in for dental surgery. Teddy is over eleven or twelve years of age, I forget which and, unfortunately, his lower teeth were rotting out. He had some teeth removed a few years ago but these were really bad. They didn't know if Teddy was strong enough to take anaesthesia, so they had to give him a cardiogram. Well, one of the most heartbreaking afternoons of my life was spent holding Teddy with two veterinary techs as the poor little guy was given a cardiogram to see if his heart was strong enough to take anesthesia in order to have his teeth extracted two days later. Well, he let out a cry during the cardiogram that was almost inaudible to anyone except me. It wasn't a howl. It was a high-pitched cry at an almost inaudible frequency—something that a whale or a porpoise might give out as a distress sound. But that's when I heard Teddy's inner voice talking to me. Well, two days later, he had to go in for this surgery—he was on the table for three and a half

"I know this: that every moment I have with Teddy is a moment I will cherish."

hours. When I got him back home that evening, naturally he was still on anesthesia, on drugs just as any human would be. He hardly recognized anything. He was listless but I brought him back to life with, believe it or not, human baby food and the greatest love I've given anyone in my life (except for my own children). As I was bringing him back from his pain and drugs, I would quietly hum to him, "Movie star, you're my movie star." He responded in the same way that my silent brother did, showing that he knew it was me. Slowly but surely I saw him come back to life, restored to the happy little guy that I have known for so many wonderful years. I don't know how many years we have left together—that's up to God, not up to me or the dentist—but I know this: that every moment I have with Teddy is a moment I will cherish.

With my "little sister" Tasha

ACKNOWLEDGMENTS

Thank you to my editor Kate Hartson,
who loved Teddy at first sight.

Many thanks also to Vince Remini
for his masterful eye.